RYAN DIXON

I0062244

TRADING
FOR
BEGINNERS

The Concise Guide For Profitably Trading
Stocks, Forex & Crypto

Crystal Swan Group Publications

First Edition, April 2024
Copyright © 2024 All Rights Reserved

Crystal Swan Group Publications
CrystalSwanGroup.com

ISBN 979-8-218-40933-3

This book is dedicated to the public education system who stated it was their job to prepare us for the future, and yet somehow, in the fifteen thousand plus hours they had our attention forgot to take even a few minutes out to teach us the fundamentals of financial literacy...

as though money would have no role of importance in the future.

TABLE OF CONTENTS

DISCLAIMER

The information contained in this book is intended for educational and informational purposes only. It does not constitute financial, investment, trading, or any other form of advice. The authors and publishers of this book make no representations or warranties of any kind, either express or implied, as to the accuracy, completeness, reliability, or suitability of this information for any particular purpose.

Trading and investing in financial markets carry a high degree of risk and may result in significant financial losses. Past performance does not guarantee future results. You should not trade or invest with any money you cannot afford to lose. Before making any trading or investment decisions, you should carefully consider your personal circumstances, trading experience, objectives, and risk tolerance. Always seek the advice of a qualified financial advisor who can take all these factors into consideration.

The strategies, examples, and techniques discussed in this book are for illustrative purposes only and may not be suitable for all investors. Markets are constantly changing, and any information provided might become outdated or inaccurate over time. The author and publishers cannot be held responsible for any losses incurred as a result of using the information in this book.

This book includes references to various financial instruments, trading platforms, brokers, and other third-party services. These references are provided for informational purposes and do not constitute an endorsement of any particular product or service. It is your responsibility to conduct thorough research and due diligence before choosing any platform, broker, or other service provider mentioned in this book. The authors and publishers assume no liability for any decisions you make based on these references.

The authors and publishers of this book may hold positions in the assets discussed within. These positions are disclosed for informational purposes and should not be construed as recommendations or advice.

You are solely responsible for your own investment decisions. The authors and publishers shall not be liable under any circumstances for any direct, indirect, special, incidental, or consequential damages that may arise in connection with your use of the information in this book or any related trading or investment activities.

PREFACE

Before we dive into this, I just wanted to take a moment to say thank you. Not only for getting this book, but for having the desire to improve your standard of living for yourself, your family, friends and those closest to you. Just about everyone has that desire, but a much smaller number will ever actually do anything about it.

I wanted that same thing, and while I initially had some misconceptions about what that process would look like, how much time and discipline it would require, and the emotional rollercoaster it would entail...my immovably persistent nature pushed me to continue. As with almost anything, patience and persistence pay. I can't stress how much of this is about self-mastery, patience, persistence and endurance. It's something you have to dedicate yourself to and decide that no matter how long it takes or how hard it gets, that you'll continue to show up, day after day after day.

If you can make that commitment to yourself, and those closest to you, then you will endure long enough to learn from experience. That learning will make you better, stronger and more skilled. And that continued improvement of skill will ultimately be what transforms you from a trader who loses most of their trades, to one who breaks even, and eventually to one who has more successful trades than not.

There are a lot of people out there who will portray trading as this quick, easy way to infinite riches. To the uninitiated, this can be a seductive influence. Typically, little warning is given by these individuals, leaving the beginner unaware of how little he knows and an exaggerated sense of being better at trading than they actually are. This can all but guarantee losses, discouragement and eventually quitting.

In an attempt to mitigate this, there needs to be an honest and transparent discussion about what to expect, what to watch out for, and how to approach trading as a beginner. I personally think it's similar to boxing. It takes skill, dedication, determination, discipline and endurance. You have to know and accept that no matter how good you get at the sport, you're still going to take a few to the head, and some of those hits will be very unpleasant. You have to be willing to take those blows, and after some time off, you have to be willing to get back in the ring and do it again, and again, and again.

Not unlike boxing one of the keys to a long career is knowing when *not* to get in the ring. As your skill set increases, you'll begin to realize when to trade and when to abstain because the markets are likely to give you "chop". Everyone knows that markets go up and down, and those are great opportunities to make money. But it's the sideways periods known as chop which even more seasoned traders prefer to abstain from. These can be considered sideways periods of movement where buyers and sellers are fairly balanced. It will typically occur after a directional trend has exhausted itself

Traders will tend to avoid these periods because they can be unpredictable, full of false signals in either direction and contain low volume. In trading you want to wait for the market to *tell* you which direction it's going rather than attempting to *predict* which direction it's going.

There are plenty of other things to be cautioned about within this book, but I thought a glimpse of what it is and isn't was a good place to start.

You should not, however, let these warnings discourage you either. Trading can be a highly profitable endeavor over the long term, not to mention a lot of fun. Furthermore, it can provide you a very useful tool when the world throws uncertainty your way. When the covid scare occurred, the majority of humans lost any semblance of logic. Unenthused at the prospect of entertaining their delusions, trading allowed us to simply disassociate almost entirely from society as we waited for things to blow over and people to come to their senses. Whether we see something like that again in our lifetimes remains to be seen, but what is certain is that life will always throw the unexpected at you. Often times, the unpleasantness of such events can be alleviated or, at the least, tamped down with a little extra capital at your disposal.

To be clear, getting into trading won't immediately let you quit your day job. Even if you begin to get good at it, you probably shouldn't quit your job. Once, however, you build up enough capital reserves and enough regular income from trading to supplement your lifestyle while still increasing your overall portfolio allocations, then at that point, it's a discussion to be had with yourself (and probably your significant other while you're at it). Depending on your situation, you may still want to keep a day job if for no other reason than to keep yourself out of trouble.

What you choose, of course, will entirely be up to you, but ultimately you will have a choice you didn't previously have. The more choices you have, the more free you are, and the value of that freedom can not be understated.

When putting this book together, I was challenged with the task of brevity. I intentionally wanted this book for beginners to be on the lighter side as far as content goes so as not to dissuade or discourage those who may be curious to explore it. The difficulty there is that brevity has not historically been a strength of mine. Those who know me are undoubtedly enjoying a good chuckle having just read that. In an effort to abate my zeal for communication I've had to be resourceful (*another trait that will serve you well in trading*), and leverage various artificial intelligence language models to help me "trim the fat" so to speak. To the creators of those models, I just want to say thank you, as it's served a useful purpose here. Without their efforts, this book would likely be the size of 'Remembrance of Things Past' by Marcel Proust.

Even greater thanks to my wife, Sarah for...well, everything really. If I had any idea how I got so lucky to have you, I'd instead have written a book on that subject so that the gentlemen of today could know a similar sense of being blessed with a truly wonderful wife in their lives. Alas, I have no clue...dumb luck I guess, sorry fellas.

As men, we're tasked with the traditional role to provide and protect. However, if the last few years have taught us nothing else, it is that life is uncertain and you never really know when your time is up. To that effect, I hope to provide some redundancy at least where provision is considered. That is to say, I wrote this in hopes that if something were to happen to me, that the contents of this book and future books in the series may be able to be leveraged by my wife in order to not be dependent on employers, rising economic conditions, or others than herself. If and when she chooses to apply herself to this endeavor, I have every faith and confidence that she will do incredibly well for herself and our children.

And while family has served as the spark and tinder for this endeavor, I can see no reason that anyone else pursuing the same should not be able to be the beneficiary. It is my hope that the contents provided herein may be used as a stepping stone for anyone and everyone wanting to improve their condition in life.

Whether you do or do not depends upon the conviction of your will.

WELCOME TO THE WORLD OF TRADING

Imagine having the ability to potentially profit from the fluctuations in the prices of stocks, currencies, or even crypto. That's the realm of trading—a world filled with possibilities where savvy decisions, a bit of understanding, and some self-discipline can bring financial rewards.

What is Trading?

At its heart, trading involves buying and selling assets with the goal of making a profit. Let's break down a few key concepts:

Financial Markets: Think of these as giant marketplaces where various assets are bought and sold. You've likely heard of the stock market (*where shares of companies like Apple or Tesla are traded*), the forex market (*where currencies like the US Dollar and Euro are exchanged*), and maybe even the cryptocurrency market (*where digital currencies like Bitcoin and seemingly endless altcoins reside*).

Buying (Going Long): When you believe an asset's price will rise, you buy it with the hope of selling it later at a higher price.

Selling (Going Short): When you think an asset's price will drop, you can sell it (*even if you don't own it yet*) with the aim of buying it back later at a lower price. Since the concept of shorting is often confusing for beginners, let's take a brief look at how it works.

How Shorting Works:

Borrowing: Imagine your friend has a video game you want to play. You could borrow it from them.
Selling: While you have the borrowed game, you could sell it to someone else for money.
Buying Back (*Hopefully Cheaper*)**:** Later, if the game's price drops, you can buy it back at the lower price.
Returning the Game: Finally, you return the game to your friend and keep the profit you made from the price difference.

Technical Analysis: The Trader's Toolbox

While some investors focus on a company's financial statements, economic news, and other fundamental analytics, traders turn to a different tool: charts! Technical analysis is the study of price charts to identify patterns and trends that can help make informed trading decisions. Think of it like a detective using clues to understand what might happen next.

A Sneak Peek

In the chapters to come, you'll learn how to read and analyze charts, uncover hidden patterns, and develop your own trading strategies. But first, let's get you set up with the most popular tool used by traders: TradingView!

Let's get started!

GETTING STARTED WITH TRADINGVIEW

Welcome to your trading toolkit! In this chapter, we'll walk through setting up a free TradingView account and unveil its essential features to kickstart your technical analysis journey.

Setting Up Your TradingView Account

Head over to www.tradingview.com and create a free account.
You can opt for a paid subscription later.
Choose your preferred registration method (*email or social media login*).
Once you're in, explore! Take a moment to familiarize yourself with the layout.

TradingView Interface Breakdown

TradingView offers a user-friendly interface that organizes everything you need for charting and analysis. Here's a quick rundown of the key areas:

Chart Area: This is the center stage where price charts come alive! You can customize it to display different markets (*stocks, forex, crypto*) and timeframes (*daily, hourly, etc.*).

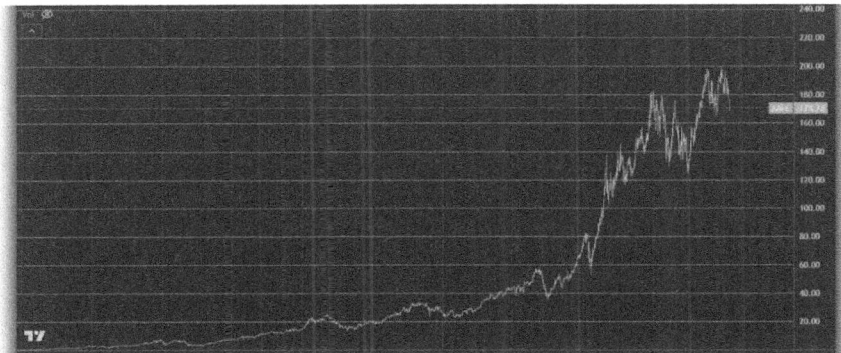

Toolbar: This handy area houses buttons for essential charting functions like adding drawing tools (*brushes, support/resistance lines, etc*), text, Fibonacci levels, and much more.

Watchlists: Organize your favorite assets for quick access and stay on top of price movements. You can create different watchlists for stocks you're interested in, frequently traded forex pairs, or the latest cryptocurrencies. Organized correctly, this section can save you a ton of time, allowing you to simply cycle through different charts by hitting the spacebar looking for attractive chart patterns, almost like flipping through channels on cable television.

Symbol Search Bar: Consider this your gateway to any asset you want to trade. Simply click the magnifying glass in the top left section, type in a crypto ticker symbol (e.g., BTCUSDT for Bitcoin paired against USDT) or a currency pair (e.g., EURUSD for Euro vs US Dollar), and start charting!

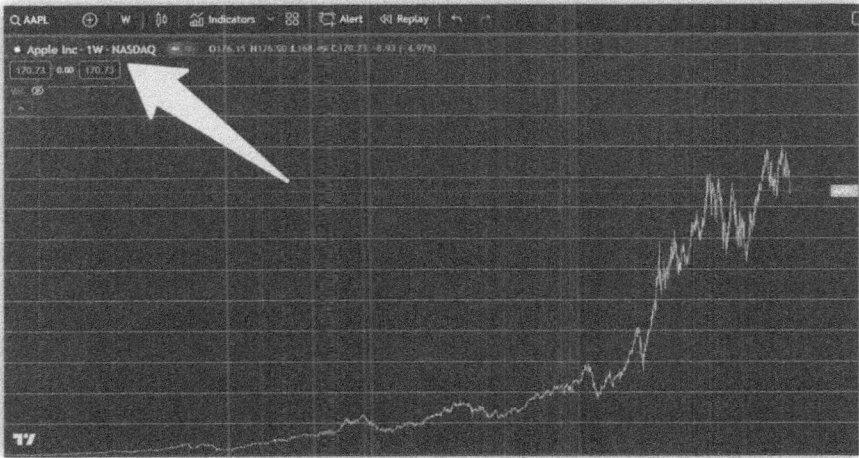

Simply click on the icon in the top right that looks like a newspaper or list. To add a stock, currency pair, or crypto, simply click the plus symbol, type the name into the search field, and then click the plus symbol on the right.

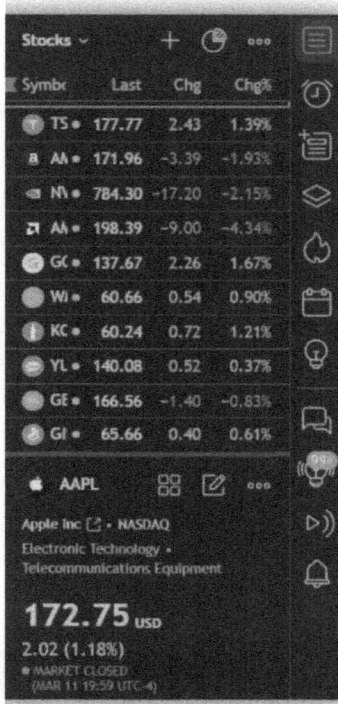

Taking Your Charts for a Spin

Let's get some hands-on experience! Here's how to navigate the chart area and customize it to your preferences:

Search for a Stock: In the search bar, type in a well-known stock symbol like AAPL (*Apple*) or TSLA (*Tesla*).

Timeframe Selection: Use the buttons above the chart to switch between different timeframes. Start with a monthly, weekly, or daily view to get a broad overview of the price movement.

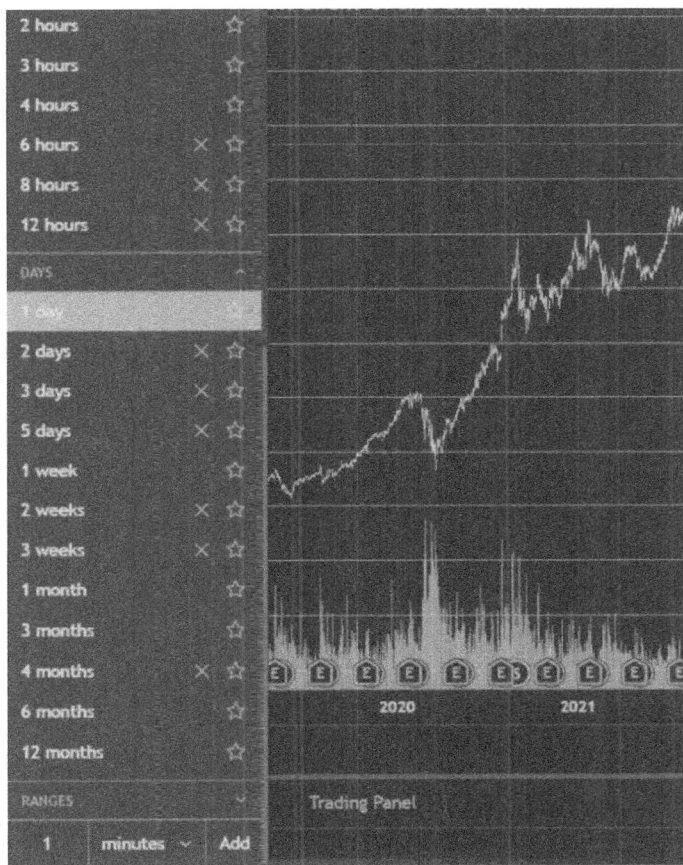

Zooming In and Out: Use different time frames to see price action more or less granularly. Click and drag the X or Y Axis along the side or bottom to pull more or less of the price action in or out of view.

Pro Tip: TradingView offers a variety of keyboard shortcuts that can make navigating the charts even faster. A list of these can be found under the Help section. Alternatively, you can visit https://www.tradingview.com/charting-library-docs/v24/getting_started/Shortcuts/ to view the tables with them listed.

Customizing Your Charts:

Chart Type: TradingView allows you to display price data in various chart types like bar charts, candlesticks (*the most popular choice for technical analysis*), or line charts. Play around and see which one you find easiest to understand.
Price Scale: You can adjust the price scale on the right side of the chart to better visualize price movements.

Chapter 2 lays the foundation for using TradingView, but there's much more to explore! In the next chapter, we'll delve into the world of candlesticks, the building blocks of technical analysis.

UNDERSTANDING CHARTS & CANDLESTICKS

Now that you're more familiar with TradingView, let's unlock the secrets of charts. In the world of technical analysis, charts are the trader's map, and candlesticks are the signposts that help you decipher price movements.

The Structure of a Chart

Think of a chart as a visual story of an asset's price over time. Here's the basic anatomy:

Price Axis (*Y-Axis*): This runs vertically on the chart, showing the price range the asset has traded within. Each tick mark represents a different price level.

Time Axis (*X-Axis*): This runs horizontally along the bottom of the chart, dividing the price history into time segments: minutes, hours, days, weeks, or months.

Trading Volume: Often displayed below the price chart, this shows how much of the asset is being bought and sold over a certain period, revealing the level of interest and activity. If volume is absent on a chart, you can bring it up by selecting it from the indicators section and simply typing in 'volume'. Volume is fundamentally important in deciphering the validity of price action and determining if it's giving bearish or bullish signals.

9

If both price action *and* volume are increasing, it can be a bullish sign. If both price action and volume are decreasing, it can be a bullish sign. However, if you see price action increasing but volume decreasing, this could be a warning sign that the recent upward movement is not as strong as it might appear and that downward action is in the cards.

Candlesticks: Your Charting Compass

Candlestick charts are the most popular choice for technical analysis. Each candlestick visually summarizes the key price action for a specific timeframe. Let's break down the anatomy:

The Body: This rectangular part shows the difference between a timeframe's opening (start) and closing (end) prices.

The Wicks (Shadows): These thin lines extending above and below the body show the highest and lowest prices reached during that timeframe.

Green or White Body: The closing price was higher than the opening price (*bullish signal*).
Red/Black Body: The closing price was lower than the opening price (*bearish signal*).

Decoding a Candlestick: A candlestick tells you a lot about whether buyers or sellers dominated the action during a particular period. Long bodies suggest strong momentum, while short bodies suggest indecision. Long wicks indicate significant price swings and volatility.

Popular Candlestick Patterns

Experienced traders learn to recognize specific candlestick patterns indicating potential trading opportunities. Here are a few examples to get a sense of this:

Hammer: A bullish candlestick with a long lower wick, a small body, and little or no upper wick. It suggests strong buying pressure after a dip.

Doji: A candlestick with nearly equal open and close prices and long wicks, demonstrating indecision in the market.

Bullish Engulfing: Two candlesticks. The first is a small red (*bearish*) candle, and the second is a larger green (*bullish*) candle that completely "engulfs" the first. This can indicate a potential bullish reversal, where buyers overwhelm sellers, signaling a change in momentum.

Bearish Engulfing: The opposite of the bullish pattern. A small green candle is followed by a larger red candle that engulfs it. This could mean a bearish reversal, suggesting strong selling pressure and a possible downward move.

Morning Star: Three-candlestick pattern. A long red candle, followed by a small-bodied candle (*can be either red or green*), and then a long green candle that measures 50% or better the length of the first candle in the pattern. Here, you have a potential bullish reversal pattern often found at the bottom of downtrends.

Evening Star: The opposite of the Morning Star. A long green candle, followed by a small-bodied candle (*either color*), and then a long red candle. This is a potential bearish reversal pattern found at the top of an uptrend, signifying a momentum change.

Important Note: Remember, the context in which these patterns appear is crucial. Always look for confirmation from other technical indicators and consider the overall trend before making trading decisions.

Pull Up a Chart: Return to TradingView and open a chart for a stock, forex pair, or cryptocurrency you're interested in. Let's start with a well-known stock like AAPL (*Apple*).
Switch to Candlesticks: Make sure the candlestick chart type is selected.

Zoom In: Choose a timeframe, like 1 hour, and zoom in to see individual candlesticks in detail. Notice the variations in body size and wick length. Try to identify various candlestick patterns and observe the subsequent price action.

Next Up

In the next chapter, we'll introduce the concepts of support and resistance, which are crucial for understanding how traders identify key price levels where potential changes in direction can occur.

INTRODUCTION TO SUPPORT AND RESISTANCE

Imagine the price of an asset as a ball bouncing around in a room. Support and resistance act like the floor and ceiling, respectively. Understanding these key levels can give you valuable clues about where the price might reverse or break out.

What is Support?

Support is a price level where buyers tend to step in, preventing the price from falling further. Here's why this happens:

Buying Opportunity: Traders may see the price drop near a support level as a bargain and start buying, creating upward pressure.

Stop-Loss Orders: Traders who've bought the asset at higher prices may have placed 'stop-loss' orders (*orders to sell if the price falls below a certain level automatically*) just below the support level, creating another source of buying pressure.

What is Resistance

Resistance is the opposite of support - a price level where sellers tend to step in, preventing the price from rising further. This occurs because:

Profit-Taking: Investors who bought the asset at lower prices may be tempted to take their profits near a resistance level, increasing selling pressure.

Short-Selling: Some traders may actively bet against the asset and try to profit by short-selling it at the resistance level.

Identifying Support and Resistance on TradingView

TradingView makes it easy to spot potential support and resistance zones on charts. Here's how:

Historical Price Action: Visually examine the chart and look for areas where the price has reversed direction multiple times.

Horizontal Lines Tool: Use the horizontal line drawing tool (*or alt + H on your keyboard*) to mark lines where the price action has repeatedly bounced up (*support*) or reversed downwards (*resistance*). Alternatively, you can use the rectangle drawing tool to draw zones where price action has repeatedly bounced up or reversed. Some support and resistance levels are fairly precise lines, but more frequently you'll see them as tight zones where price action reacts to historical buying and selling activity.

Notice how the price action repeatedly bounces off the lower rectangular zone and repeatedly gets rejected from the top one? An important thing to remember is that previous resistance will act as support. Once the price finally breaks through the ceiling, it comes back down to test and see if it now holds as support. Once the market confirms the previous resistance as support, it knows where the new floor is, so it heads upwards to find the new ceiling.

Types of Support and Resistance

Historical Levels: Prices where the asset has reversed direction in the past. These levels often act as psychological barriers. (*pictured above*)

Trendlines: Diagonal lines that connect a series of higher lows (*uptrends*) or lower highs (*downtrends*). These act as dynamic support or resistance. Notice how the previous (*top*) diagonal resistance also acts as support once broken.

Moving Averages: Popular technical indicators that smooth out price data. They can sometimes act as support or resistance. We'll cover these in a future chapter. For now however, just observe how frequently price action bounces off this simple 200 moving average.

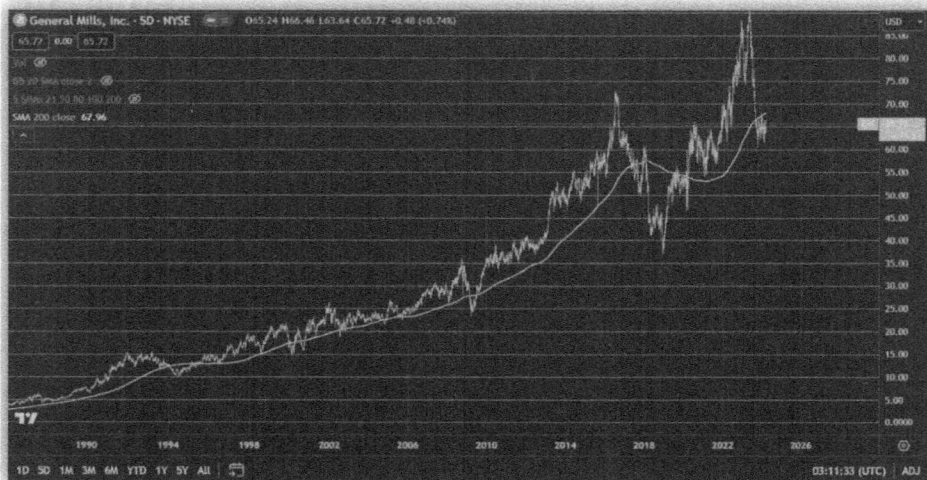

Key Points to Remember

Support and resistance levels are not always precise. Think of them more like zones rather than exact price points. Instead of drawing lines, some traders prefer using the rectangular drawing tool to represent where these zones are on the charts visually.

Support can turn into resistance if a price breaks down through that level, the same way that resistance can turn into support if the price breaks above it!

Practice Makes Perfect

Pull up a few charts in TradingView and use the horizontal line tool and/or rectangular box drawing tool to identify potential support and resistance levels. Start with longer timeframes (*daily or weekly*) to spot the most significant zones. Remember that support and resistance zones from decades ago can extend into price action today! Once you've gotten a handle on horizontal levels, explore diagonals similarly.

Coming up next:

Understanding entry styles, strategies, traps and risk management.

MASTERING ENTRIES: STRATEGIES, TRAPS, AND RISK MANAGEMENT

Timing your entry is critical to maximizing profits in trading. This chapter will explore common entry methods, how to recognize potential traps that could ruin your trade and the importance of setting strategic stop-losses.

Common Entry Strategies

- **Breakout Trading:** Entering a trade as the price breaks above a resistance level (*bullish breakout*) or below a support level (*bearish breakout*).

- **Example:** Imagine a stock has been trading between $20 and $25 for weeks, with at least three prior rejections at the $25 level. A breakout trader might wait for a surge in volume accompanying a decisive break above $25, indicating strong buying pressure. Keep in mind that all breakouts are fakeouts until they aren't, however.

- **Refined Entry:** To target a more reliable breakout entry, a trader can wait for the price to retest the broken resistance level (*now acting as support*) and confirm its validity. This retest often provides a lower-risk entry point than the initial breakout but with potentially less reward.

The illustration below shows that gold was rejected at around the $2,000 level for several years. The more conservative entry would be to wait and see if previous resistance holds as support. Once price action provides a higher-term time frame closure above the dotted line (*where price action initially broke out to before coming down to retest the previous resistance*), enter a long position.

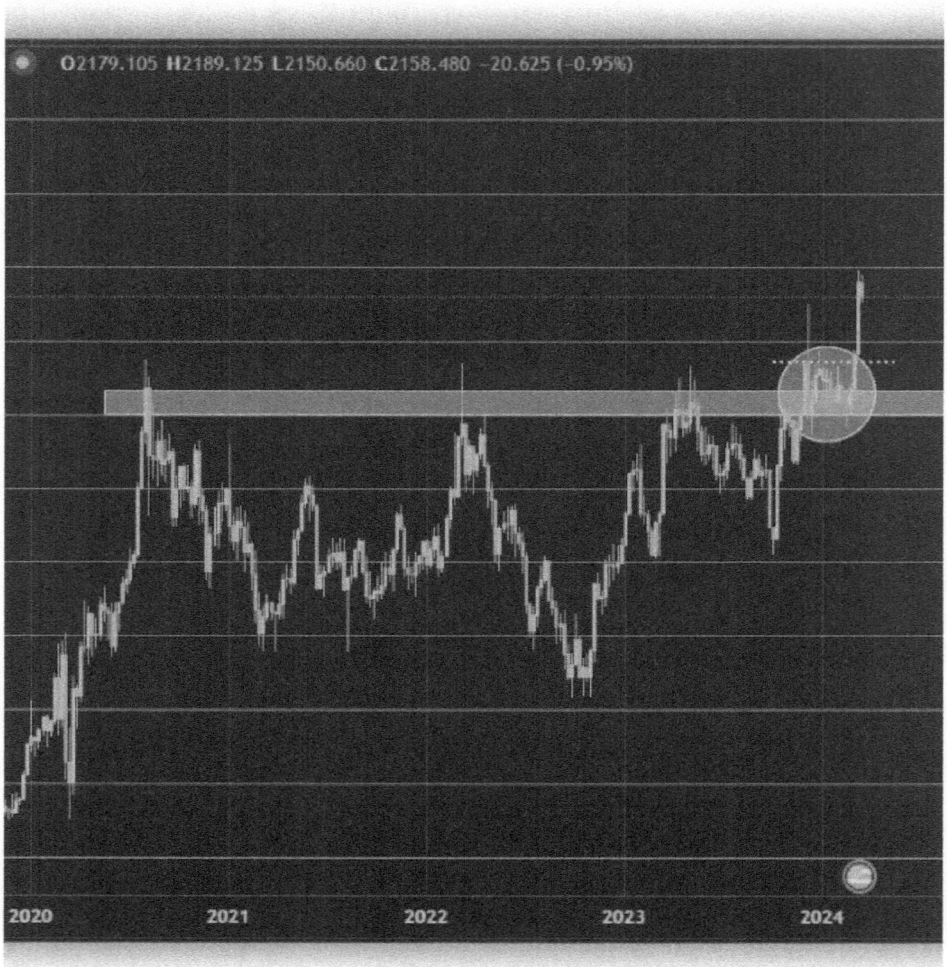

Key Points:
Look for high-volume spikes on breakouts for confirmation.

- Look for confluence from technical indicators to strengthen the breakout signal. Think of confluence like supporting evidence in a court case, where you are the judge. The more supporting evidence you have, the more certain you can be about your decision.

- Retests offer potential entry zones but be aware of false breakouts (*bull traps/bear traps*). Side note: *traps can offer some of the most lucrative trading opportunities if you identify them early and can act quickly to countertrade them.*

- Decide between a more aggressive entry at the retest or a safer one after the price confirms support and closes above the breakout zone.

- Breakouts can occur on larger and smaller term time frames.

- **Buying Support/Selling Resistance:** Entering a long trade when the price bounces off a known support level, or a short trade when the price is rejected at a resistance level.

- **Example:** If a stock consistently bounces off the $50 level, a trader employing the support strategy might look to buy near this area if the price returns there again.

The Dangers of Bull and Bear Traps

- **Bull Trap:** Occurs when a breakout above resistance *fails*, leading to a sharp reversal to the downside. Traders who bought the breakout get trapped in a losing position.

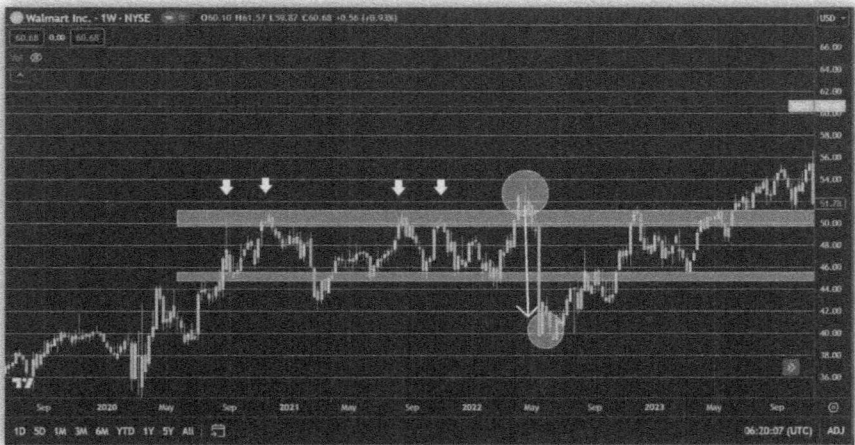

- **Bear Trap:** The opposite of a bull trap. A breakdown below support fails, leading to a sharp reversal upwards Traders who sold short on the breakdown get trapped. Notice price respected the S&R zone numerous times before it failed to bounce at support. A trader might open a short position here, only to get trapped as the price then swings all the way back up again.

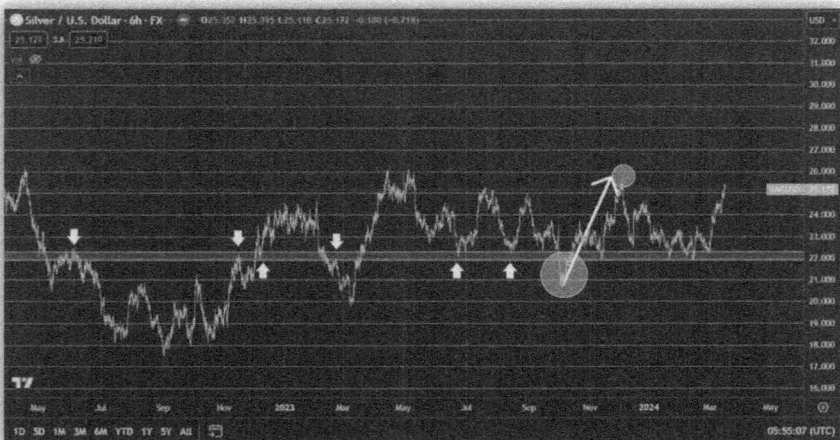

Protecting Yourself: Counter-Trading and Stop-Losses

- **Counter-Trading the Trap:** If you suspect a bull or bear trap, you can try to reverse your position quickly, minimizing losses and potentially profiting from the reversal. However, this requires good timing and decisive action.

- **Strategic Stop-Losses:** A stop-loss order is an essential tool for any trade. It automatically sells (*for long positions*) or buys back (*for short positions*) your asset if the price moves against you by a certain amount. Setting a stop-loss below a support level (*for longs*) or above resistance (*for shorts*) can help limit your loss if a trade goes wrong.

Beginner Tips

- **Observe and Practice:** Watch charts and identify breakout levels, support/resistance zones, and potential traps.

- **Volume Matters:** Look for increased volume to confirm breakouts and support/resistance bounces.

- **Never Risk Too Much:** Use stop-losses and position sizing to manage risk, especially when you're less certain about a trade setup.

Coming Up Next

Understanding where and how to enter is essential, but we've only scratched the surface! In the next chapter, we'll introduce one of the most powerful tools in a trader's arsenal – technical indicators.

TECHNICAL INDICATORS: YOUR CHARTING POWER-UPS

Technical indicators are like superpowers for your chart analysis. They are mathematical calculations based on historical price and volume data that help traders identify trends, measure momentum, and generate potential buy or sell signals.

Types of Technical Indicators

The world of technical indicators is vast, but we can break them down into a few main categories:

Trend Indicators: These help determine the overall direction in which an asset's price is moving (*uptrend, downtrend, or sideways*). Popular examples include Moving Averages, MACD, and ADX.

Momentum Indicators: These measure the strength or speed of price movements, often hinting at potential overbought or oversold conditions. Examples include RSI (*Relative Strength Index*) and Stochastic Oscillator.

Volatility Indicators: These gauge how much the price of an asset swings up or down, giving insights into market sentiment and potential turning points. They can be very useful for knowing when to expect volatile swings however, they don't tell us what direction the swing will be. A classic example is Bollinger Bands.

Volume Indicators:

Traders use volume indicators to gain deeper insights into the strength and conviction behind price movements. Here's a look at two important types:

Volume: This standard indicator displays the raw number of shares or contracts traded in each time period (*e.g., hourly, daily*), often as bars located below the main price chart. Traders analyze volume to:

Identify Trend Strength: High volume during an uptrend or downtrend suggests strong momentum.

Spot Reversals: Declining volume during a trend might signal weakening momentum and a potential reversal.

Confirm Breakouts: A volume surge accompanying a price breakout can indicate strong conviction behind the move.

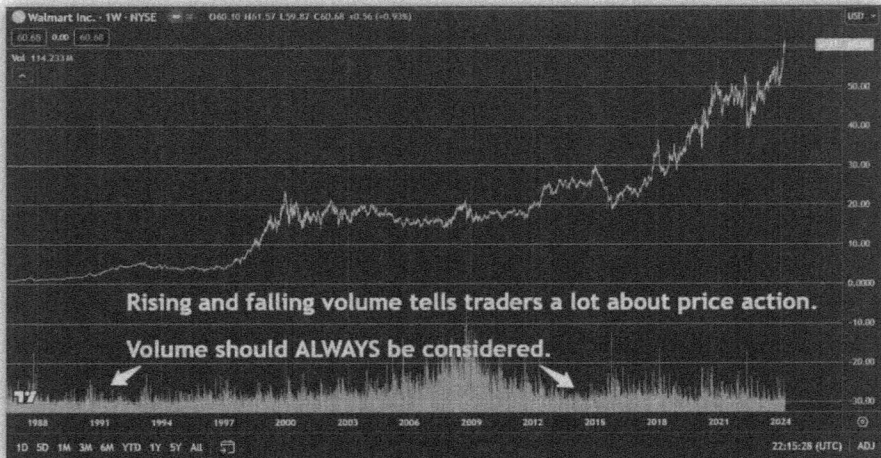

Rising and falling volume tells traders a lot about price action. Volume should ALWAYS be considered.

Volume Profile Visible Range (VPVR): This indicator creates a histogram along the price chart, showing the volume traded at each price level over a specified time. This helps traders identify the following:

Areas of Support and Resistance: High-volume nodes often signal areas where traders are actively buying or selling, which can correspond to support and resistance levels.

Potential Breakouts: A surge in volume above a high-volume node could indicate a strong breakout.

When using VPVR, changing the 'Row size' setting to 200 is recommended to gain a more granular visual of volume ranges. Additionally, as you play with this indicator notice how it changes based on what portion of the chart is in view. That's because it's actively computing volume for the areas you show it. Some traders will use a zoomed-out view of the charts paired with this indicator to determine where to enter and exit trades. Price action going above a large volume region into a low volume zone can indicate an entry. Running out of a low-volume zone into a high-volume region can help determine where to exit.

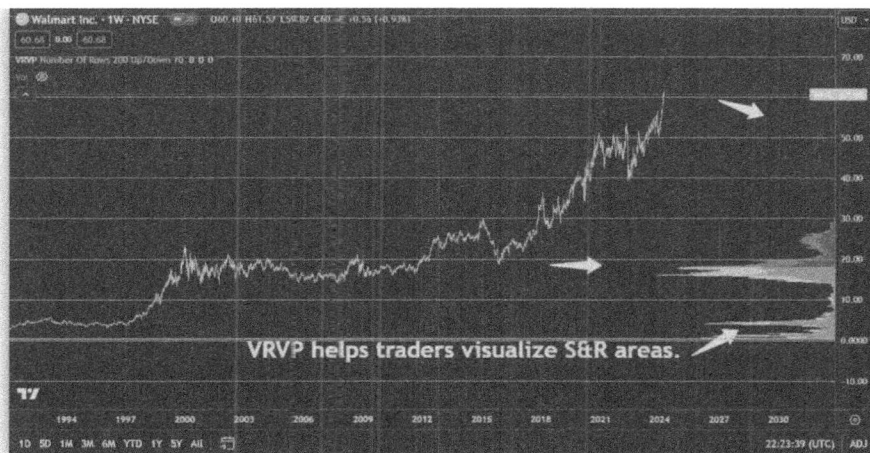

VRVP helps traders visualize S&R areas.

How to Use Technical Indicators in TradingView:

TradingView offers a massive library of built-in technical indicators. Here's how to add them to your charts:

Click the "Indicators" Button: It looks like a little bar chart icon in the toolbar above your chart.

Search for an Indicator: Type in the name of the indicator you want to use (like "RSI" or "Moving Average").

Adjust Settings: Most indicators allow you to customize inputs and parameters. For example, changing the period for a moving average will change its calculation.

Important Note: No single indicator is perfect. It's best to combine several indicators to get a more complete picture of a trade setup.

Popular Indicator Examples

Next, let's look at two widely used indicators:

Moving Averages (MA): Simple trend-following tools that smooth out price data. When the price is above a moving average, it may suggest an uptrend; when it's below, it may suggest a downtrend.

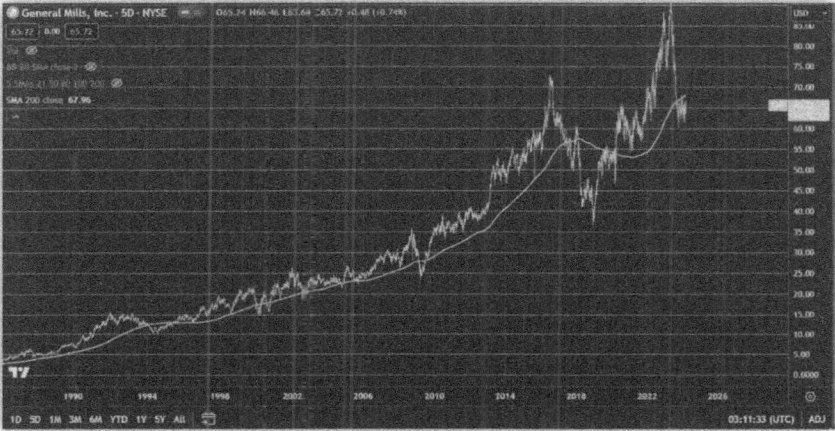

Relative Strength Index (RSI): A momentum indicator oscillating between 0 and 100. Values above 70 might indicate overbought territory, while values below 30 might indicate oversold territory. Some traders even *exclusively* use trend lines on the RSI to execute positions!

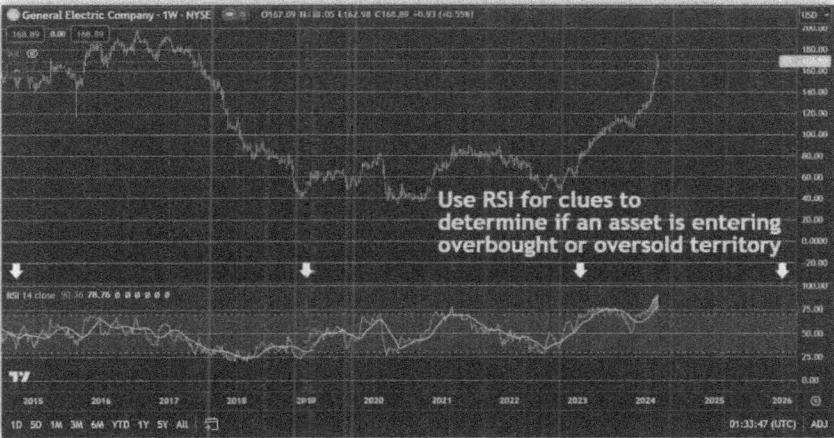

Use RSI for clues to determine if an asset is entering overbought or oversold territory

Practice Time

Pick a Popular Indicator: Choose an indicator like the RSI or a Moving Average.

Experiment: Add it to various charts on TradingView. Try different timeframes and asset classes (*stocks, forex, etc.*).

Observe: Notice how the indicator reacts to price movements. Can you spot any potential trading signals it generates?

Popular Indicator Examples (*With Setups*)

Let's explore how two popular indicators can be used in practice:

Moving Averages (*MA*) for Trend Trading:

Setup Example: Add a 20-period Simple Moving Average (*SMA*) and a 50-period SMA to your chart. When the short-term (*20-period*) SMA crosses above the longer-term (*50-period*) SMA, it may signal a potential bullish trend. Conversely, when the short-term SMA crosses below the longer-period SMA, it may signal a bearish trend.

Caution: Moving average crossovers can provide a directional view but can generate false signals in sideways markets.

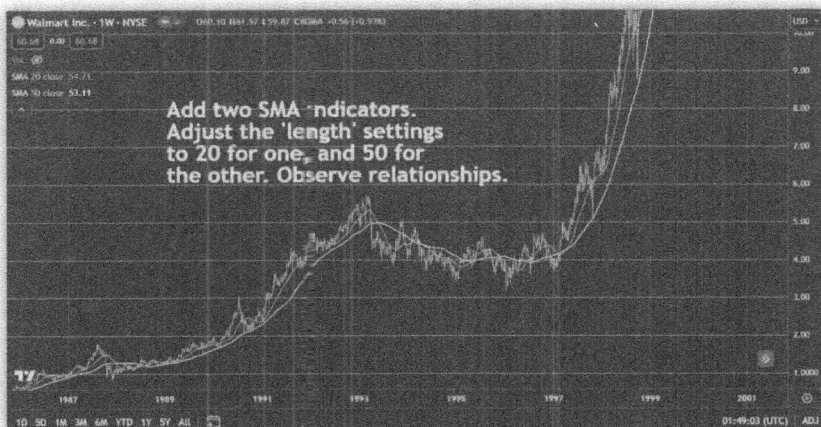

Add two SMA indicators.
Adjust the 'length' settings
to 20 for one, and 50 for
the other. Observe relationships.

Relative Strength Index (RSI) for Overbought/Oversold:

Setup Example: When the RSI crosses above 70, it might indicate an asset becoming overbought and a possible price reversal. When the RSI dips below 30, it can signal an oversold condition and a potential bounce.

Caution: Overbought/oversold signals don't necessarily mean an immediate price reversal. They are best used in combination with other indicators or chart patterns.

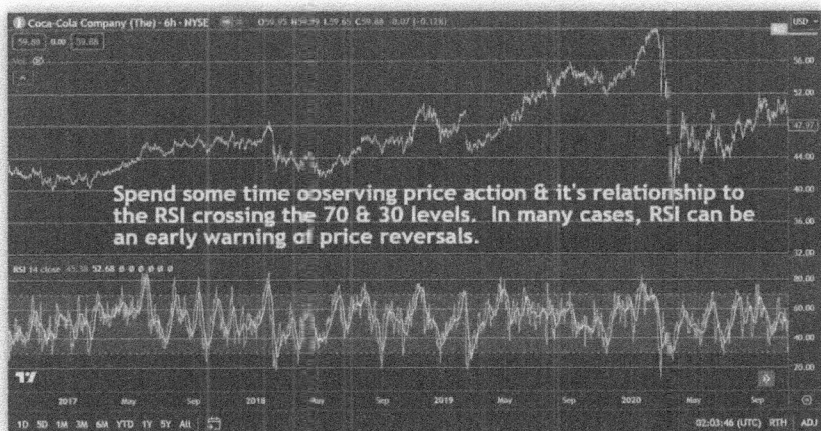

Spend some time observing price action & it's relationship to
the RSI crossing the 70 & 30 levels. In many cases, RSI can be
an early warning of price reversals.

Practice Time

Backtesting: Go back in time on a chart and add combinations of the Moving Average and RSI indicators. See if you can identify potential crossover setups or overbought/oversold conditions that preceded significant price moves.

Important Reminders

No Single Holy Grail: Avoid relying on any indicator blindly. Technical indicators offer clues, not guarantees.

Confluence is Key: Always look for multiple indicators and factors lining up to strengthen your trading ideas.

Next: Applying Your Knowledge

Now that you've gained a solid understanding of charting tools, support/resistance, and indicators, it's time to develop a deeper understanding of technical analysis. In the next chapter, we'll discuss how to put all these pieces together!

Words of Caution

Technical indicators are powerful, but they can also be misleading at times. Remember:

They are lagging: Indicators are based on past price data, so they may not always accurately predict future price movements.

They are subjective: Different traders may interpret the same indicator differently.

In the next chapter, we'll discuss how to combine the knowledge you've acquired about charting tools, support and resistance, and indicators to solidify your understanding of technical analysis.

BRINGING IT ALL TOGETHER: DEVELOPING YOUR TECHNICAL ANALYSIS SKILLS

Thus far, you've built a solid toolbox of technical analysis knowledge. You know how to read charts, identify support and resistance, and use technical indicators. It's time to combine these concepts to develop your trading strategies.

Key Steps in Technical Analysis

Identify the Market Trend: Is the asset in a clear uptrend, downtrend, or trading sideways? Moving averages or trendlines can be helpful here. Think of the trend as the direction in which the river is flowing. You can swim against it (placing shorts in an uptrend or longs in a downtrend), but generally, you'll be better served to go with it.

Locate Support and Resistance: Identify key levels where the price has reversed in the past. These levels can offer clues about potential entry or exit points.

Look for Confirmation: Use technical indicators to back up your analysis. Are indicators like RSI or MACD supporting the trend direction you've identified? Do they suggest momentum is strengthening or weakening?

Manage Your Risk: Where will you place your stop-loss order for protection if the trade starts moving against you? Where will you take full or partial profits? Technical analysis tools can help you set these levels strategically.

Example: A Swing Trading Entry

Let's use an example to illustrate how this process might look:

Asset: Bitcoin

Timeframe: Daily Chart

Trend: Price action has established a series of higher highs and higher lows. Additionally, the price is above the 20-period and 50-period moving averages, further confirming an uptrend.

Support: The price has bounced several times off a horizontal support level near $25,500.

Indicator: The RSI is above 50, confirming bullish momentum.

Trade Idea: Consider buying Bitcoin if it pulls back to the support level near $25,500 to $26,000 with a stop-loss order placed just below the support level.

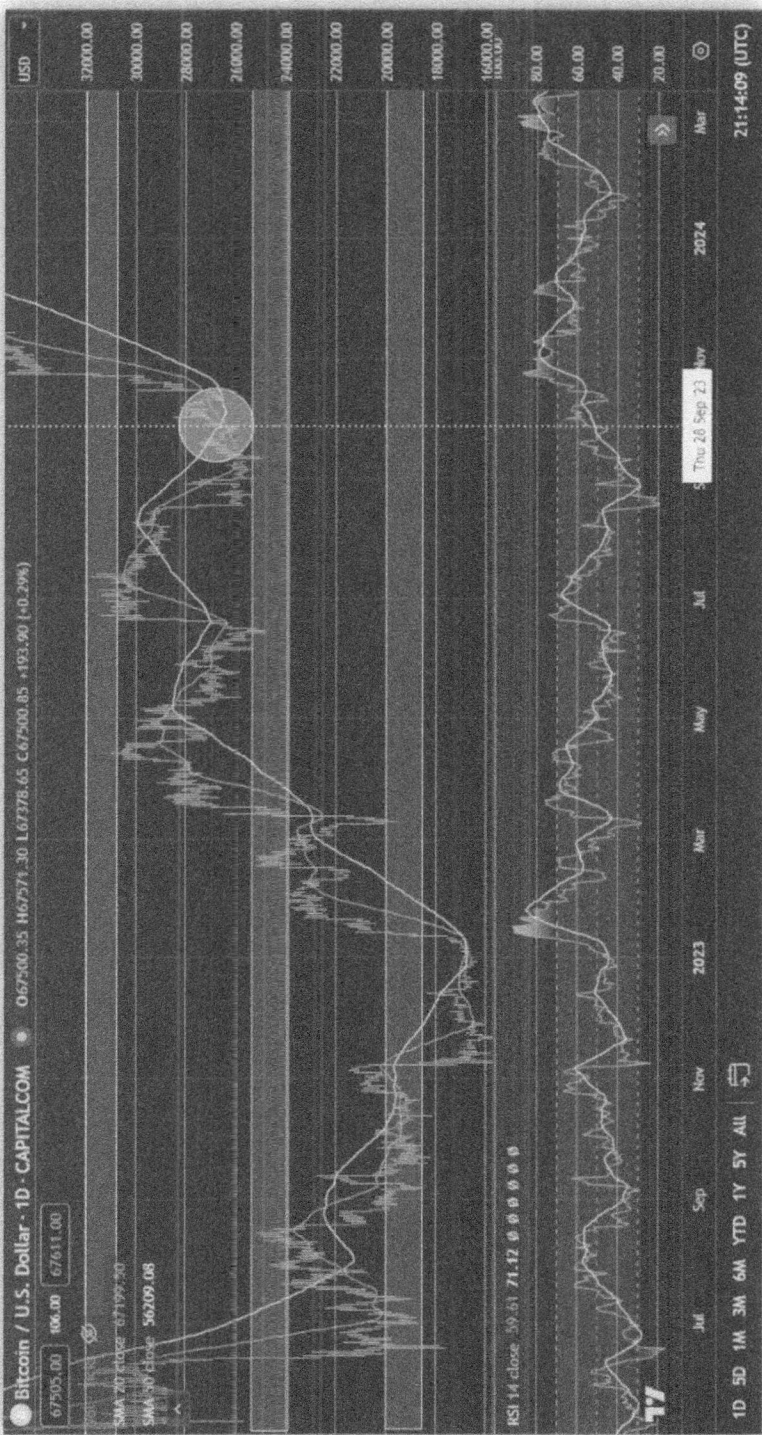

41

Developing Your Own Process

This is just one example; over time, you'll develop your preferred methods. Here are some additional tips:

Start with Simplicity: Focus on mastering a few key indicators and chart patterns before diving into complex strategies.

Backtest Your Ideas: TradingView makes it easy to go back in time on a chart and test how your trading setups would have performed historically.

Keep a Trading Journal: Record your trades, your reasoning behind them, and the outcomes. This will help you identify your strengths and weaknesses.

Technical Analysis is an Art and a Science

Trading involves both technical analysis skills and the psychology of managing risk and uncertainty. While the tools we've discussed can greatly enhance your decision-making, they are not foolproof.

Next Steps: Your Learning Continues

We've only scratched the surface of technical analysis! It's a vast discipline with countless strategies and techniques to explore. In the upcoming chapters, we can delve into:

More advanced technical indicators

Specific candlestick patterns and their implications

Trading psychology and risk management strategies

ADVANCED TECHNICAL INDICATORS

While foundational indicators like RSI and Moving Averages are invaluable, a whole universe of more sophisticated technical analysis tools is waiting to be explored. Let's introduce a few that can add another dimension to your trading decisions:

MACD (*Moving Average Convergence Divergence***):** This versatile momentum indicator helps gauge the strength of a trend and potential turning points. It comprises two moving averages of different lengths and a histogram representing their difference. Here's how it works:

Crossovers: When the faster-moving average line (*blue by default*) crosses above the slower line (*red by default*), it may signal a bullish trend shift. A crossover below may indicate a bearish turn.

Divergence: When the MACD line makes a lower high, but the asset price makes a higher high, this divergence may signal weakening momentum and a potential reversal.

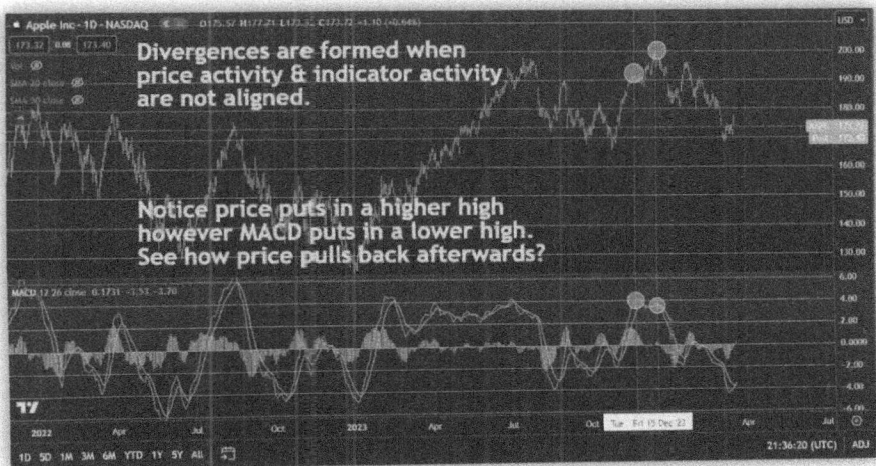

Bollinger Bands: These dynamic bands visually depict price volatility around a center line (*which is usually a moving average*).

Range Trading: When price moves within the bands, it could indicate a range-bound market. Breakouts above or below the bands can signal trend shifts.

Squeezes: When the bands narrow (*low volatility*), it can suggest a period of consolidation and a potential breakout is coming.

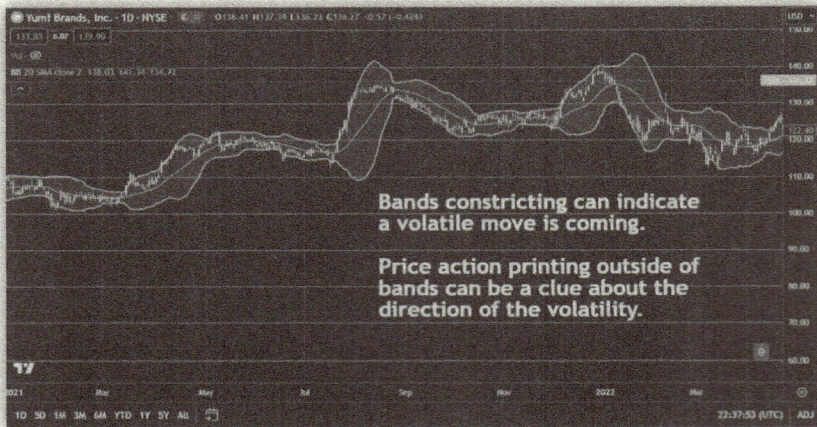

Bands constricting can indicate a volatile move is coming.

Price action printing outside of bands can be a clue about the direction of the volatility.

Stochastic RSI: Remember the Relative Strength Index (*RSI*), the oscillator that helps identify potentially overbought and oversold conditions? The Stochastic RSI takes this concept a step further.

- **How It Works:** Stochastic RSI applies the Stochastic Oscillator formula to the output of the standard RSI. This adds a layer of calculation, aiming to make overbought/oversold signals more refined.

How to Use It:

- **Crossovers:** Like other oscillators, look for crossovers of the Stochastic RSI lines for potential buy/sell signals. The 'K' line (*blue by default*) crossing above the 'D' line (*red by default*) can indicate potential long opportunities, while the inverse can be true for shorts when it crosses below.

- **Extremes:** Values above 80 generally signal overbought conditions, while values below 20 suggest oversold conditions.

- **Important Note:** Stochastic RSI, like all oscillators, can give false signals, especially in choppy or sideways markets. Always consider it alongside other indicators and forms of price analysis. You can also use this indicator to look for divergences between price action & indicator action. Divergences can hint at potential reversals on the horizon.

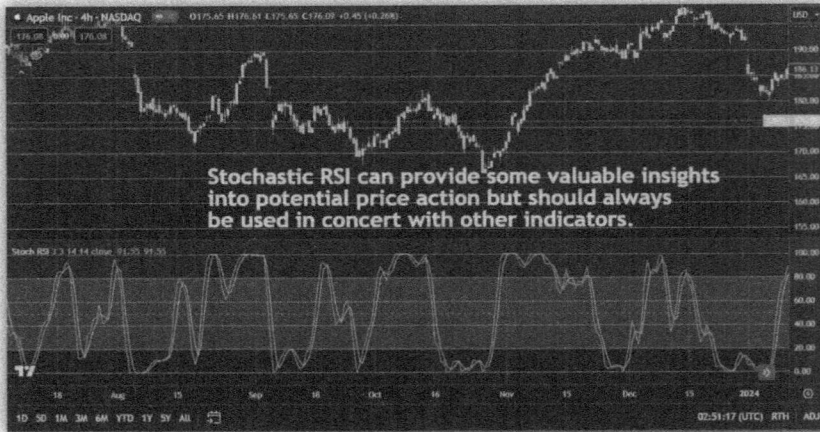

Stochastic RSI can provide some valuable insights into potential price action but should always be used in concert with other indicators.

Practice Time: Adding Indicators to Your Chart

Experiment in TradingView: Add the abovementioned indicators to a chart and observe how they change with different price movements.

Combination Analysis: Try combining these advanced indicators with the basics you've learned earlier (*RSI, moving averages*). Can you identify any setups where multiple indicators align?

Remember Your Foundation

While advanced indicators can be powerful, always keep those fundamental concepts in mind:

Trend Identification: Is the overall trend up, down, or sideways (bouncing up and down inside a tight range)?
Support and Resistance: What major price levels are providing potential turning points?

A Word of Caution

Even the most complex indicators aren't foolproof. Use these tools to confirm your analysis, not dictate it entirely. Always consider the broader market context and remember proper risk management techniques.

Next: Mastering Candlestick Patterns

Technical indicators are powerful, but for the discerning trader, there's an even more ancient art to master: the language of candlestick patterns. In the next chapter, we'll explore these chart patterns and how to interpret their signals.

MASTERING CANDLESTICK PATTERNS

Candlestick patterns offer a visual shorthand for understanding market psychology and potential price action. By learning to recognize these patterns, you can gain valuable insights into the struggle between buyers and sellers.

Popular Bullish Candlestick Patterns

In previous chapters, we discussed some of the more popular candlestick patterns traders look for to help them identify potential directional shifts in price action.

Stepping Up Your Candlestick Knowledge:

- **Inverse hammer:** This is a single candlestick pattern similar to the hammer we discussed earlier. The main difference is that instead of a small body located at the top and a long wick underneath, this one has a small body with a long upper wick. It can indicate buying pressure that was met with selling pressure; however, the selling pressure was not strong enough to continue to force the price down further.

Three White Knights: A strong signal that bullish momentum is picking up. This three-candle signal typically reveals itself at the bottom of downtrends and consists of three consecutive green or white candles, each with little to no wicks, which open and close progressively higher.

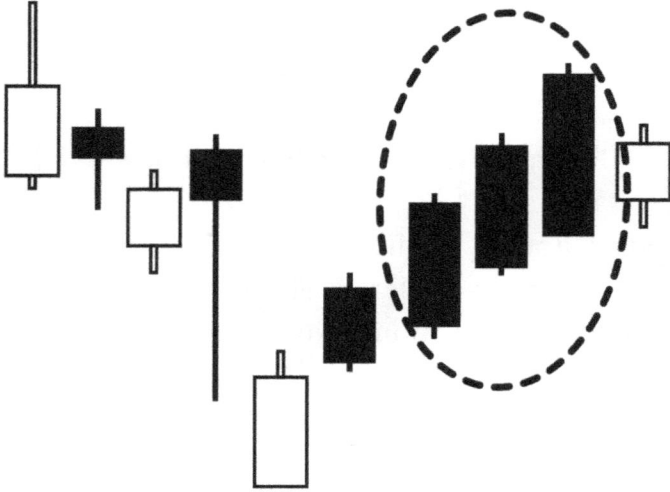

Three Black Crows: This bearish pattern is similar to the Three White Knights pattern; however, it is comprised of red or black candlesticks and is often found at the top of an uptrend or as a continuation signal in a downtrend.

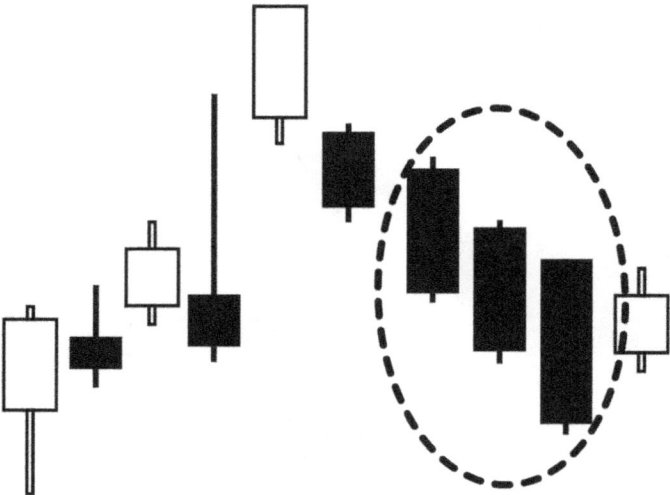

Harami: While this single candlestick pattern isn't typically enough to open or close a trade on, it can be an early warning signal for traders that the current trend may be losing momentum. The harami can be bullish or bearish and consists of a small candle body that fits entirely inside the previous candlestick body. Look for the bullish harami at or near support zones, and the bearish harami at or near resistance levels.

Harami Cross: A Harami Cross is very similar to the Harami and can have the same implications for traders. The main difference is that instead of a small body fitting into the previous body, we find a small doji candle during an up or down trend. This can indicate indecision and a possible reversal.

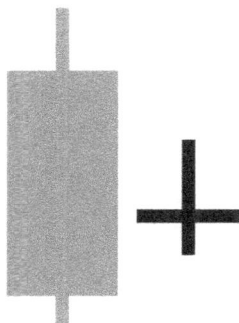

Remember, Context is King:

While these patterns offer valuable insights, it's important to remember some key points:

Confirmation is Key: A single candlestick pattern shouldn't be the sole deciding factor in your trades. Look for confirmation from price action, changes in volume, or other technical indicators to strengthen the pattern's validity.

Consider the Trend: The location of the pattern within the overall trend matters. A reversal pattern near a support or resistance level often carries more weight than one in the middle of a strong trend.

False Signals Exist: No candlestick pattern is foolproof. The market can sometimes throw "false signals" that lead to unexpected moves. Use these patterns probabilistically and always have stop-loss orders in place to manage risk.

Chart Exploration: Pull up charts of various assets in TradingView and switch to the candlestick display. Start with well-known stocks.

Pattern Hunting: Try to identify bullish and bearish candlestick patterns discussed above.

Look for Confluence: Do they occur near key support or resistance levels? Do indicators like RSI confirm the signal?
Next Up: Psychology & Risk Management

Chart patterns and indicators are powerful, but successful trading also depends on understanding human psychology (*including your own*) and managing risk effectively. In the next chapter, we'll dive into these crucial aspects of trading

TRADING PSYCHOLOGY & RISK MANAGEMENT

Technical analysis is a powerful tool, but it's only half the battle. The other crucial factors for trading success are having the right mindset and implementing effective risk management strategies.

Trading Psychology: The Mental Game

Fear and Greed: These powerful emotions can lead traders to make impulsive or irrational decisions. Recognizing when they influence you is a crucial first step to controlling them.

Overconfidence: A string of winning trades might lead to taking on excessive risk. Always remember that the market can (*and will*) turn against you anytime.

Discipline: Sticking to your trading plan is essential, even when faced with emotional turmoil.

Strategies for Managing Emotions

Know Yourself: Analyze your past trades and emotional reactions. Do you tend to make rash decisions in the heat of the moment, or do you struggle to cut losing trades?

Journaling: Writing down your trades and the thought processes behind them can help you identify patterns in your behavior.

Breaks and Mindfulness: Regular breaks from trading can help manage stress levels, and mindfulness exercises can improve your composure in the face of volatility. Additionally, trading higher-term time frames can help reduce the time you spend glued to your charts.

Risk Management: Protecting Your Capital

Risk management is about managing the downside of trading. No matter how good your strategy is, there will always be losing trades. Here are some vital principles:

Position Sizing: Never risk more than a small percentage of your capital (*2% or less per trade is a decent starting point*) on any single trade. This prevents a bad trade from completely destroying your account. Remember, trading is a marathon, not a sprint!

Stop-Loss Orders: These essential orders automatically exit your trade once a specific price level is reached, limiting potential loss. In almost all cases, you'll want to have a stop-loss order set to prevent liquidation losses.

Risk-Reward Ratio: Aim for trades where your potential reward outweighs the risk. A risk-reward ratio of 1:2 or higher is a good rule of thumb. However, it's not uncommon for traders to use a 1 to 1.5 risk-to-reward ratio. Use the 'long position' (*or short position*) tool located in the toolbar on the left to help you measure out your entry, take profit, and stop loss levels.

Example: Setting a Stop-Loss

Let's say you're buying stock XYZ at $100. After analyzing the chart, you decide your stop-loss should be at $95, limiting your risk to $5 per share. If you invest $1000, you will purchase 10 shares to keep your total risk in line with your risk tolerance.

Trading is a Marathon, Not a Sprint

Successful trading is all about consistency and calculated risk-taking. Developing your trading psychology takes time and self-awareness. By implementing effective risk management strategies, you'll protect your capital and trade more confidently.

Further Exploration

There's always more to explore, and numerous resources can help you deepen your understanding of trading psychology and risk management. Future books will have more on risk management as well.

Next: Putting it All Together

We've covered a lot of ground, from charts and technical analysis to trading psychology. In our final chapter, we'll discuss how to synthesize these concepts into a practical trading process.

PUTTING IT ALL TOGETHER – YOUR TRADING PROCESS

Congratulations! You've built a solid foundation in technical analysis, candlestick patterns, trading psychology, and risk management. Now, it's time to integrate it all into a structured approach that aligns with your individual trading style.

The Importance of a Trading Plan

A trading plan is your roadmap to success; it helps make disciplined decisions when facing market volatility. Here are essential elements to consider:

Your Trading Style: Are you a day trader, swing trader, or position trader? Your trading style will dictate your ideal timeframes and holding periods.

Preferred Markets: Do you want to focus on stocks, forex, cryptocurrencies, or other markets?

Entry Criteria: What specific technical analysis patterns, indicators, or setups will trigger you to enter a trade?

Exit Criteria: When will you take profits? Under what conditions will you close a losing trade?

Risk Management: How will you determine your position size and where will you place your stop-loss orders?

Record-Keeping: What metrics will you track in your trading journal to identify areas for improvement?

An Example Trading Plan (Simplified)

Style: Swing Trading
Market: Large-cap US Stocks.
Entry Criteria:
Price crosses above the 20-day Moving Average, confirmed by RSI above 50.
Bullish Candlestick Pattern (hammer, engulfing, etc.) forms near support.
Exit Criteria:
Target Profit: Sell half on a 2:1 risk-reward ratio. Trail a stop-loss for the remainder. (*More on trailing stop losses in a future edition of this series*)
Stop-Loss: Set stop loss just below a significant support level.
Risk Management: Risk 1% of capital per trade.

Continuous Improvement

Your trading process is not set in stone. As you gain experience, you'll refine your plan and tailor it to your unique strengths and risk tolerance.

Backtest Your Ideas: Using historical data, use TradingView to backtest your trading process. This will give you a sense of how it might perform under different market conditions.

Review Your Trades: Regularly analyze your trading journal to identify recurring patterns in wins and losses. Do you notice any strengths or weaknesses that need attention?
Resources and Next Steps

Your learning journey is just beginning! Here are a few resources to help you continue growing as a trader:

Trading Communities: Forums, social media groups, and online courses can connect you with other traders to learn and share ideas.
Books on Trading: There are many excellent books on specific trading strategies, risk management, and market psychology.

Paper Trading: Practice your process with a paper trading account (*simulated trading*) to gain experience without risking real capital.

Remember: Trading success is about discipline, continuous learning, and adapting to changing market conditions.

Thank you once again for beginning your trading journey. While most people just wish for an improvement in their conditions, you are actually taking actionable steps towards that goal!

As discussed in the preface, if you are committed, resilient, and determined, you will achieve what you set your sights on. Remember that it is a journey and you will have wins and losses along the way.

If you want to do yourself a favor, heed the words in this book. It can be exciting and tempting to jump head-first into trading, but you'll have better results taking things slowly at first and exercising caution. Over time you'll build up your skill set and be able to trade larger position sizes for bigger wins. For the time being, try your hand at paper trading to gain practice without assuming any actual risk. And if you are going to risk actual capital, take seriously the risk management techniques discussed in this book.

In the next book, we'll expand more on what you've already learned, and by the end of it, you may be ready to try your hand at a few small trades.

Until then, be well & keep learning.